START EXPLORING
Wildlife
BE A WILDLIFE DETECTIVE!

Terry Jennings

Illustrated by Patricia Papps

CONTENTS

Headway · Hodder & Stoughton

Be a wildlife detective!

Are you a wildlife detective? Wildlife detectives look for clues to help them discover wild animals. A wildlife detective finds out where animals hide, what they eat and where they have their young. This book contains lots of activities that will help you to become a wildlife detective.

The only other things you need are your eyes, ears, nose and hands. You also need to be able to ask questions. What made this footprint? Where is that snail going? When do butterflies come out? Can you find out the answers to questions like these?

All you need to become a wildlife detective are a notebook and pencils. Collect some plastic pots with lids and some small plastic bags. A magnifying glass or hand lens is useful for looking at tiny animals. A plastic spoon and a soft paintbrush will help you to pick up small animals without hurting them.

3

Making a start

Wherever you live, there are many animals to be found. Almost every little space outside is a home for a small animal. There are even some animals living inside your home.

Carefully search every nook and cranny, indoors and out. Peep in cracks in fences. See what is under stones and pieces of wood. Look under heaps of dead leaves. Look in the soil. Search the bark of tree trunks. Use your hand lens to help you see very tiny animals.

In your notebook write down the names of all the small animals you find. Don't forget that birds are animals, too. Say where and when you found each animal.

Again, try not to disturb the animals. Put back any stones or other objects exactly as you found them.

Now You See

What small animals are moving about your garden at night? Make a simple trap like the one opposite and find out.

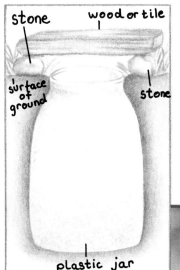

stone   wood or tile

surface of ground   stone

plastic jar

Let the animals go when you have looked at them. Dig up the trap as soon as you have finished with it.

Look at the trap every morning and evening. What kinds of small animals do you catch? Do different animals live under a hedge or a tree? What happens if you put tiny pieces of food in the trap?

5

Who has been here?

A lot of larger animals only come out at night. Although you may not see them, you can see where they have been.

Look at muddy paths, snow, wet sand and around puddles for animal tracks and footprints. The picture on these pages shows footprints made by different birds and animals.

You can often tell whether an animal walks, hops or jumps by looking at its tracks. A rabbit hops along. It often uses the same path each day. Field voles and bank voles scurry along.

squirrel

field vole

rabbit

bank vole

Some birds hop, some walk and some run. Robins and sparrows hop along, so their footprints are in twos. The tracks of ducks are easy to tell. This is because their feet are webbed. They make a footprint shaped like a triangle.

mallard

AMAZING FACTS!

The animal which makes the most footprints is a millipede, which lives in the United States of America. It has 750 feet.

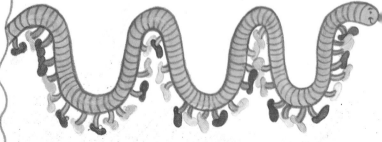

Now You See

robin

Help the birds and other animals to make some tracks. Fill a tray with sand or fine soil. Rake the top smooth. Put some breadcrumbs around the tray.

Watch to see which animals come to feed. When one has walked on your tray, look at its footprints. Draw one of each kind in your notebook.

Who has been eating here?

When we have been eating we leave behind bits of food and wrappings. Often you can tell what kinds of animals have been about by the clues they leave behind.

Search under pine trees for cones. Have any of them been eaten? A squirrel has been eating this pine cone.

Look under hazel trees for eaten nuts. A squirrel splits a nutshell into two neat halves.

A wood mouse makes a round hole in a hazel nut. You can see the mouse's teeth marks.

You may find a hazel nut fixed to the bark of a tree. A nuthatch put it there. The bird will later peck a hole in the shell to eat the nut inside.

Some squirrels use a tree stump as a table. Can you find a squirrel's table like this?

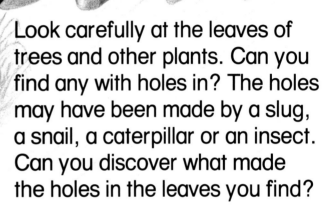

Look carefully at the leaves of trees and other plants. Can you find any with holes in? The holes may have been made by a slug, a snail, a caterpillar or an insect. Can you discover what made the holes in the leaves you find?

Look out for empty snail shells as well. Broken snail shells near a large stone show where a thrush has been feeding. The thrush breaks each shell open on the stone. Then it eats the animal inside.

AMAZING FACTS!

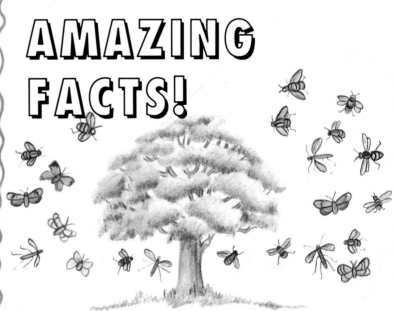

About 500 different kinds of insect feed on oak trees.

Favourite foods

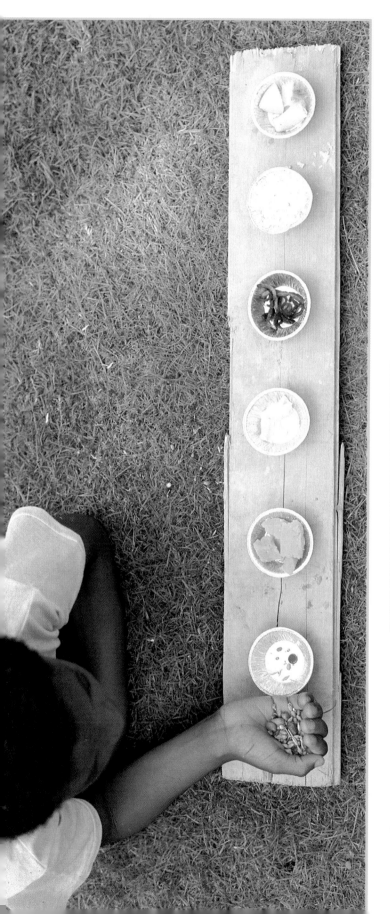

What is your favourite food? Why do you like it? Does it taste or smell good? Does it look nice? Is it good for you?

We eat lots of different foods. But most animals eat the same foods day after day. Rabbits eat mostly grass and leaves. Spiders eat flies and other insects. Even so, like us, animals have favourite foods.

Find out which foods birds like best. Fix 5 or 6 tin lids to a small plank of wood. Lay the plank on the ground where you can see it. Make sure it is away from trees and bushes where cats could hide.

favourite foods

breadcrumbs	fat
III	₊ₕₜ
seeds	cheese
II	III
potato	bacon rind
IIII	II

Put a different food in each lid. Some foods you could try are breadcrumbs, fat, seeds, cheese, cooked potato and little pieces of bacon rind.

See how many birds go to each lid.
Which lid is empty first?
Which food do the birds like best?
Which do they like least?
Now try other foods.

Who has been visiting these flowers?

Have you seen bees going to flowers in the garden? The bees go to collect the yellow dust called **pollen**. They also collect sweet nectar from the flowers. What other kinds of insects can you see going to flowers?

Garden flowers are all shapes and colours. Which colour do bees like best? Watch some flowers for about half an hour. Count how many bees go to each colour flower. Which colour flower do most bees go to? Do flies and butterflies like the same colour that bees do?

Now You See

Make a flower out of tissue paper. Put a tiny speck of honey in the middle of it. Stand your flower among some real flowers.

AMAZING FACTS!

When butterflies stamp up and down on a leaf they are 'tasting' it to see if it is the right kind to lay their eggs on.

How to make a paper flower

1 Cut out some circles of tissue paper.
2 Put them all together and pinch the paper to a point in the centre.
3 Now separate the circles out from each other so that they look like flower petals.
4 Attach your flower head to a green garden cane or something similar. You can stick some leaves on as well if you like.

Minibeast mobile

1 Cut out all the pieces of the mobile around the thick black lines. Fold each piece along the dotted lines, glue the non-printed sides together and leave to dry.

2 Ask an adult to help you pierce a small hole, shown by a circle, in each piece.

3 Position one of the cross bars at right angles to the other one. Thread a piece of string or wool 25 centimetres long through the holes in the middle of each cross bar. Secure it underneath with a knot. (You might find it easier to keep the two cross bars at right angles if you stick a small piece of Sellotape where they overlap.)

4 Thread 4 pieces of string 30 centimetres long through the holes punched in the insects and secure them with a knot. Attach the dragonfly and the butterfly to opposite ends of one cross bar, and the bee and ladybird to opposite ends of the other.

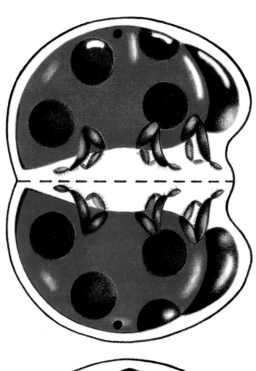

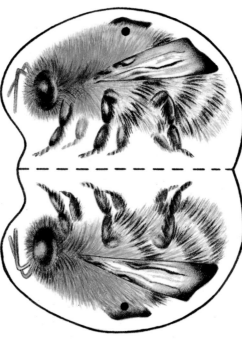

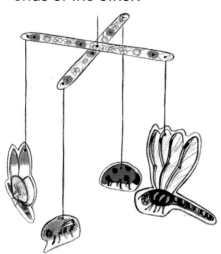

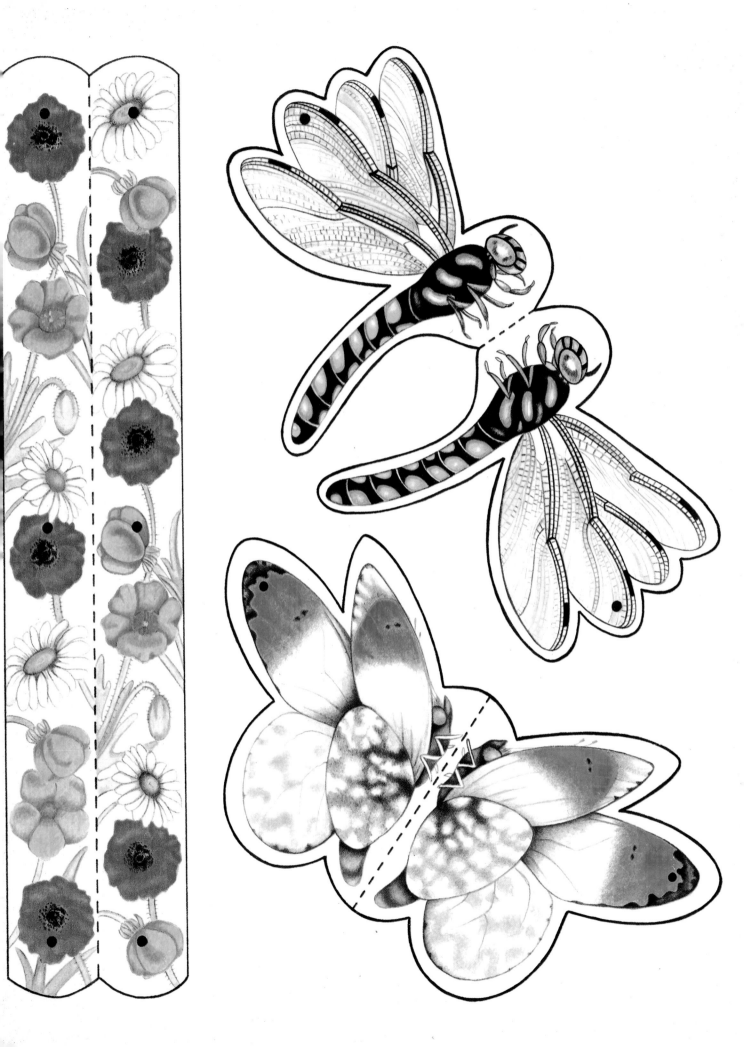

Do any insects come to
your flower?
What kinds are they?
Make flowers of other colours.
What colour do insects like best?

Bath time

All animals, like people, need water. Animals need water to drink and sometimes to keep themselves clean. Make a bird bath. Then you can watch the birds bathing and drinking.

Find a shallow dish or, even better, an old dustbin lid. Sink it in the soil. Make sure that it is away from trees and bushes. Fill your bird bath with clean water.

Which kinds of birds come to your bath? How many of them drink? How many of them bathe? Do all birds drink and bathe in the same way?

date	bird	bathing or drinking	weather
3rd June	robin	bathing	warm and sunny
"	gold finch	drinking	warm and sunny

AMAZING FACTS!

Although most animals have to drink water, the jerboa or desert rat does not. It gets water from the food it eats.

What is the weather like when the birds bathe or drink? Keep a record like the one above. Do any birds bathe in very cold weather? Do any other kinds of animals use your bird bath?

Now You See

Some birds don't like to bathe in water. Instead they bathe in dust.

Use a large shallow box to make a dust bath. Put it in a sunny place. Fill the box with a mixture of dry sand and dry fine soil. Sprinkle a few breadcrumbs around your dust bath. What kinds of birds come to the bath?

In wet weather cover the dust bath over to keep it dry.

15

Who lives here?

Like people, many animals have a home. It may be a nest, or a hole or burrow. An animal is warm and dry in its home. It is safe from its enemies. Babies are also born in an animal's home.

Look carefully for holes, burrows and nests. Do not go too near birds' nests in spring or summer. If you do, the birds may leave their eggs or babies to die.

AMAZING FACTS!

A badger's home is called a **sett**. One of the largest badger setts ever found had 94 tunnels. Badgers had been using it for 250 years.

Holes in the ground 15 to 20 cm across are made by rabbits. A much larger hole may belong to a badger.

Holes 4 or 5 cm across in a dry bank usually belong to a mouse or vole. If the hole is in a river bank it may be the home of a kingfisher or water vole.

Look carefully at a lawn. Are there any tiny holes in it? Can you find out what made them? Go out in the garden when it is dark with an adult. Take a torch with you. Can you see which animals live in the holes in the lawn?

Now You See

In the spring, birds often cannot find materials for making their nests. This is how you can help them.

Collect dry grass or moss and short pieces of wool. Save carpet fluff and the fur from cats and dogs when they have been combed. Put them all in a large net bag. Hang the bag up on the branch of a tree.

What kinds of birds come to the bag? Which materials do they take?

Life in a shell

Lots of animals in the sea live in shells. A snail also lives in a shell.

Search for snails first thing in the morning and when it has been raining. Look under stones, bricks, logs and pieces of concrete and metal. Always put the things back gently in the same place.

Now You See

Find a snail in the garden. Carefully mark its shell with a felt-tipped pen. Remember where the snail was hiding. Move the snail about a metre away. Each day see if it has gone back to where you found it. If it has, try moving the snail even further away. Can it still find its way home?

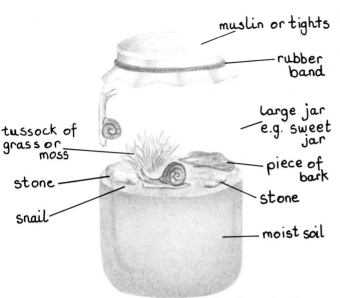

muslin or tights
rubber band
Large jar e.g. sweet jar
piece of bark
stone
moist soil

tussock of grass or moss
stone
snail

Insert cabbage or lettuce leaf as food.

A desert snail was sent from Egypt to the British Museum in London. It was fixed to a piece of card. Four years later, the snail moved. When water was put on it, it came out of its shell and ate a piece of cabbage.

You can keep a snail in a large sweet jar or plastic box for a few days. Set up the jar or box like the diagram above. Give the snail fresh lettuce or cabbage every day. Take out the old food. Watch your snail feed. How much does it eat in a day?

Wait until the snail comes out of its shell. Touch it gently with a piece of grass. What happens?

Watch your snail move up the side of the jar. What do you notice?

Put your snail on a piece of black paper. Watch it move. Can you see the silvery slime trail it makes? Can you find any snail slime trails out in the garden? Where do they go to?

Let your snail go again where you found it.

19

Camouflage

Many large animals eat smaller ones. Because they have so many enemies, small animals are often the same colour as the places where they live so they are hard to see. We say the animals are **camouflaged.**

In the summer, lay a big sheet
of plastic under the branch of a
tree. Tap the branch sharply
with a stick. Small animals will
fall down onto the plastic. How
many animals are there? What
colour are they? How many of
them are the same colour as the
leaves or twigs of the tree?
Gently put the animals back in
the tree when you have finished
looking at them.

Cut out some animal shapes.
Colour some green and some
brown. Put a green animal
against a brown piece of paper.
Is it easy or difficult to see?
Now try a green animal against
green paper and a brown animal
against brown paper. Are the
animals easy or difficult to see?
Try other colours.

Collecting the evidence

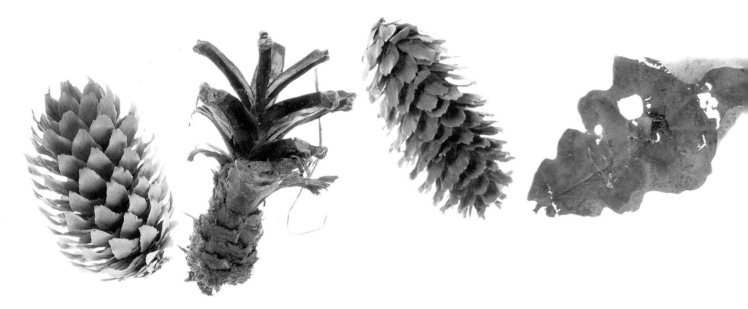

Make collections of all the clues you can discover about animals in your garden or local park.

Draw pictures of animal footprints. Colour them. Cut out the shapes and stick them on sheets of paper. Say which animal made each footprint.

Make a collection of food remains. Collect eaten nuts, pine cones and snail shells. Glue them neatly onto sheets of card. Say which animal ate each kind of food.

Press eaten leaves between layers of newspaper. When they are stiff and dry, stick the leaves on sheets of card. Say what ate each leaf.

In the autumn and winter look for old birds' nests. Wear gloves and carefully collect one of the nests. Leave it in a shed or garage for a week or two to dry.

Then, still wearing gloves, take it to pieces and see what is was made of. Do not touch birds' nests in the spring or summer, though. The birds will still be using them.

Draw pictures of animal homes you discover. Colour your pictures.

Look for bird feathers. Make collections of clean feathers. Use sticky tape to fix the feathers on a sheet of card or in a scrapbook. Say what kind of bird each feather came from.

How good a wildlife detective are you?

One snowy night a chicken was stolen from Farmer Green's shed. This is the farm the next day. Follow the clues. Who stole the chicken? How did the thief get into the shed? Where did he take the chicken to? Where is the thief hiding now? Why do you think the chicken was taken?